PUBLISHED *by* **PARABLES**
Earthly Stories with a Heavenly Meaning

Dawn of A New E. R. A.

Exciting Realm of Angels

Dr. Etienne M. Graves Jr.

PUBLISHED *by* PARABLES
Earthly Stories with a Heavenly Meaning

_____

Dawn of A New *E. R. A.*
Dr. Etienne M. Graves Jr.

Published By Parables
September, 2019

ISBN 978-1-951497-01-9
Printed in the United States of America

Readers should be aware that Internet Web sites offered as citations and/or sources for further information may have been changed or disappeared between the time this was written and the time it is read.

Dawn of A New E. R. A. Exciting Realm of Angels

Dr. Etienne M. Graves Jr.

PUBLISHED by PARABLES
Earthly Stories with a Heavenly Meaning

Contents

Dr. Etienne M. Graves Jr.

Introduction

There are certain points in history where an era ends, and a new era begins. Many times when this occurs, the brand new era is accompanied by occurrences that are foreign and unparalleled to the preceding period. We are at that point in history now. The dawning of a new age is among us. It will be an exciting realm of angels. A domain where the angelic activity will be at an all-time high. A season where the spiritual movement will overwhelm the natural world, and it will result in affecting the natural world like no other time in our existence.

Unfortunately, Christianity and many religions have remained ignorant of the many different types of angels that exist and to their operation. In this book not only is the realm of angels exposed, but the varieties of angels and angelic beings are explained in simple detail.

This book describes many of my personal experiences with angels, angelic beings, the spiritual world, and the supernatural in general.

Don't be left behind wandering in an expired era, while the excitement, power, and availability of a new period exists. Be prepared, enlightened, and in expectation of a new era. An exciting Realm of Angels.

Dawn of New E. R. A.

Exciting Realm of Angels

Dr. Etienne M. Graves Jr.

Chapter I

Out Of The Box

"For the earnest expectation of the creature waiteth for

*the **manifestation** of the sons of God."*

-Romans 8:19

We have embarked on the Dawn of a New ERA. This season is for those who are ready and willing to come out of the box of religion, tradition, and stale moves of God of the past. God always has a remnant that is positioned and prepared to not only come out of their box of the flesh and vain repetitions, but also, to remove the box that they have placed God in. Outside of this box is the realm of "anything's possible." And I do mean anything! A time when the Lord will baptize the natural with the supernatural. We will experience things that the Angels and Saints of God have never seen before. But we will have to come out of the proverbial box to work together with them.

On December 19, 2015, at 11:11 pm, after praying on my knees for only about 3 or 4 minutes, something unforgettable happened to me as soon as I got into bed. I closed my eyes for one second. I wasn't even close to falling asleep yet, and I wasn't exhausted. The next thing I know I saw in the spirit in an open night vision (*Daniel 7:13*). It was **SO REAL!!** I am trembling as I delineate this episode. I looked, and I saw the vampire, *Maximillian* (A shape-shifting Nephilim), from the film, *"A Vampire in Brooklyn,"* by Eddie Murphy.

As it seemed like I was going to confront him, to my right, out of impenetrable darkness, I saw and heard a door open (*Revelation 4:1*). **S-C-R-E-A-C-H-**. It sounded as though it had not been opened in ages. The door was ancient and venerable. I saw some holy, living creature standing by the outside of the door, like a porter or doorkeeper. But out of the door stepped a distinguished, mighty, no-nonsense looking man. He had grayish-white hair and a medium length beard of the same tone. His skin was a copper brown color as if had been burned in much time spent in the hot sun. He wore a burgundy, colored, cloak or mantle. I began to speculate, who was he?

I heard a voice, that I know to be the Holy Spirit say, "That's MOSES!" As I gazed and fixed my eyes on him as he progressed forward out of the door, He looked right at me. It was like he saw me. As he walked towards me, I heard roaring, booming, ear-splitting peals of thunder and I saw flashes of lightning surround and encase him (*Exodus 20:18*), brighter than I've ever seen.

There were not just flashes of lightning, but lightning bolts. It permeated the atmosphere with sounds of a power plant or a million electric lines running simultaneously. I started physically shaking, and trembling, uncontrollably. It was like touching an electrical socket. I couldn't take it I was scared out of my wits (Hebrews 12:21). Then He came and looked at me face to face (*Exodus 33:11*) as close as you can put your hand in front of your face. I lost it! I felt the awesomely terrifying powerful anointing on this man. I was never in any pain, but my body would not stop quaking. The closer he came, the stronger it was. Then suddenly, he turned and left and went back through the door and I opened my eyes. I shook the entire night after that. I still shudder when I think about it.

I had been asking The Father God to visit me face-to-face as He did Moses for many years. After this, I remember thinking, Wow! If I couldn't withstand the power that surrounded Moses, how could anyone EVER stand in the presence of the Father God? I have gained such an honor and respect for the prophet Moses. Not for that unprecedented, atomic electric power he had to accompany him. But I respect the humility, sacrifice, and dedication Moses had to God. I was both thrilled and terrified at the same time. I now realize that Moses wore the Fear of God like it was a cloak or a mantle.

Why did Moses come in the vision? Moses never said a word. Was it that I was not ready? He came out of hiding. Out of the box so to speak. I have been praying and searching the Word of God for an explanation of this encounter. I have learned much from the Holy Spirit about a new ERA that we are beginning.

Moses and the Spirit of the Fear of God is a major proponent in this New movement of God.

I asked the Lord why isn't there anyone walking in this tremendous anointing and power of the Prophet Moses? It was so overwhelmingly incredible. There is no doubt in my mind that this type of power dispels out hospitals and raises the dead! This power engulfs a realm, and anything or anyone that comes near it must succumb to it.

You see part of the problem is that too many believers are trying to emulate the superstar, famous preachers of today. But they don't walk anywhere near this power. Those superstar preachers mimicked the moves of great men of God of the past, to hopefully manipulate God into doing what he did for them. The vast group of believers will not enter into this new era, in the same way as the Israelites could not enter the promised land. The term for this group would be "*copycat*" or "*paper doll cut-out*" Christians. Exactly who are the "*paper doll cut-out* Christians?

"The "paper doll" Christians copy one another by using standardized methods of ministry employed in the church, or they attempt to reproduce the kind of ministry that was effective in the life of a famous minister of the past. They may try to duplicate the conditions that brought revival at another location. This use of patterns and formulas is actually a form of divination (a method of obtaining results in the spiritual realm without God's help), which He will not tolerate. Satan will often supply some of his limited power to this occult practice to advance his evil purposes. The false prophets in the Old Testament would repeat each other's words or pronounce prophecies that God had not given them (Jer. 14:14; 23:30; Ezek. 22:28).

The Pharisees obeyed complicated rules and rituals of behavior, but their reverence for God consisted of tradition learned by rote (Isa. 29:13). The Lord refused to copy both the customs of the Pharisees and the God-inspired fasting of John the Baptist (Luke 5:33). He listened and watched for His father's instructions moment by moment (John 5:19-20, 30)."- page 145, - Notes-, Anna Roundtree, The Heavens Opened).

To move into the new dimension, we must relinquish the old aspect. It's not about how much money or successful a ministry appears, how much power is the ministry walking in? That power that was on Moses is only for the true sons of God. That includes you who are reading this. However, the sons of God are in hiding, inside of the box. The whole universe and all of creation are waiting for us to emerge.

The Word of God says *11. And he gave some apostles; and some prophets; and some evangelists; and some pastors and teachers; 12. For the perfecting of the saints, for the work of the ministry, for the edifying of the body of Christ: 13. Till we all come into the unity of the faith, and of the KNOWLEDGE OF THE SON OF GOD, unto a perfect man, unto the measure of the stature of the fullness of Christ." - Ephesians 4:11-13.*

Did you notice that underlined word, *SON*? Jesus gave the five-fold ministry to train us up until a certain point. The Father is looking for manifest sons in this new ERA.

If we cling to the ministries and methods of the past, we will not be manifest sons. Many Christians will not stand in this new glory because of their tradition, but their time may come later. We must loose, ourselves

9

from past religious traditions, old forms, ceremonies, means, and methods.

There can be no hanging on of the past. There must be a clean break away from the old orders of men and God Himself. We can't adopt an ancient rule of church systems into the new order of the kingdom and sonship.

The manifestation of the sons of God will not come through those waiting for a rapture to whisk them away. The results of the expression of the sons of God will blow our minds and defy everything we have ever learned about the particular ministries of any kind.

The sons of God will not minister out of talent, natural ability, personality, charisma, or theological training; but in power and demonstration of the Holy Ghost. The sons of God will do what the Lord did after His resurrection.

You see, opposed to what we have been taught; Sons do not come as beggars, pleading, and crying, and requiring that God do for them. It is through faith and our relationship as sons and daughters that we have the privilege of asking whatsoever we will. The Son who rushes to the Father, demanding, GIVE me, give me, do this, do that, may not receive because his/her attitude is wrong, selfish, and imposing. The son who honors, adores, loves, obeys, appreciates, thanks, and eulogizes (bless) the Father, may ask what he will and receive freely.

Sons do not demand; instead, they WORSHIP, and all their needs are met in the overflow!!! Authority represents commanding. Begging constitutes requiring, and a false belief of entitlement. It's sort of like having a pet. A pet does not respond to pleading and begging, and neither do angels and demons. They react to the person with whom they are familiar with because they have the authority. Unfortunately, us believers can't break out of the box because we keep a stronghold of our P.E.T.'S. on a leash.

Dr. Etienne M. Graves Jr.

Chapter II

No P.E.T.'S. Allowed

*"Therefore **pride** (ornament with arrogance) compasseth them*

*about as a **chain** (a collar, a chain with a necklace);*

violence covereth them as a garment."

- *Asaph – Psalm 76:3*

I saw a vision, and it was of the outside of a church, but the church was made entirely from bricks. There were cars everywhere, so apparently, the brick church building was full. However, there were no doors or windows. No entry points. I saw that the Holy Ghost was trying to get into the Church to deliver people and set them free. I sensed that He wanted to do something entirely new, but He could not get in. He turned away grieved at being rejected, a sign above the Church caught my eyes. It read, *"P.E.T.'S. Allowed."*

The Lord said to me, *"son the sign on the Church should have read, "No P.E.T.'S. Allowed." I could not get into the Church to do what I want to do because of their P.E.T.'S."* I asked, *"What are P.E.T.'S?"* He said, *"P.E.T.'S. are Pride, Ego, Tradition, and Sin. Believers hold on to these weights like pets on a leash, and because of those pets, some of them cherish it.*

For this reason, I am not welcomed in and even blocked from the congregation. Even when my children are convicted and want to repent, renounce, and rid themselves of their P.E.T.'S., they are met with the same resistance as the brutal Pharaoh who enslaved the Hebrews. P.P.E.T.A. steps in to coerce and force them to keep their P.E.T.'S. and not to get rid of them."

I asked, *"PETA (People Against Unethical Treatment of Animals)?"* The Holy Ghost said, *"No. The P.P.E.T.A. I am referring to is Prophets Pastors, Evangelists, Teachers, and Apostles. Some of them are mired in Pride, their Ego's, operate by tradition and commit secret sin. They conduct their plans and agenda to keep my children dependent on them and keep them stuck in the moves of the past. I am the Living God, And I do New Things. If I Am Allowed to."*

To allow the Holy Spirit to move in our lives let's identify these P.E.T.'S. so that we can eliminate them for once. If any members of P.P.E.T.A try to hinder; then it is time to shake the dust and move on to somewhere else, where Holy Ghost is allowed to bring truth, freedom, and deliverance.

PRIDE:

What does the Bible say about pride? Pride is defined by the Bible as pompous arrogance. It must be terribly significant because Ezekiel says, *"Behold this was the iniquity of thy sister Sodom, pride, fulness of bread, and abundance of idleness was in her and her daughters, neither did she strengthen the hand of the poor and needy" (Ezekiel 16:49).* Of all that we know about Sodom and Gomorrah the first thing that we think of is homosexuality and immorality. But Ezekiel mentions pride first and foremost.

Pride is rooted in something we possess, have accomplished, an ability, or a gift. The people of Sodom had pride because of the fruitfulness of their land and how their society flourished. They felt that they were entitled to anything and everything that they wanted, regardless of whether or not it was forbidden. Even if it was banned, and was strange flesh, like men sleeping with men, which is still an abomination before the eyes of the Lord. When we believe we are entitled to something, Pride roams free like a bull in a China shop. The violence at gay Pride festivals boasts through anger.

Let me give an example of how pride manifests itself through anger. Many years ago, when my Mom worked at the LAUSD, she had a coworker who was also one of her close friends. One year, this teacher discovered she had cancer. As my mother was praying and interceding for her, the Lord showed my Mom a vision of the Christian teacher dressed as a witch for Halloween. The Lord told my Mom that if the teacher would repent and renounce this act, then He would HEAL her.

It seems like a simple act for a rewarding healing, doesn't it? But Pride reared its ugly head. The teacher was offended and began to spread hatred and rumors about my Mom around the school. She said that my Mom told her the Lord gave her cancer because she dressed like a witch. She said that my Mom said that it was all her fault and she brought it on herself. None of that was true. My Mother simply told her what the Lord said out of love. But she never repented and simmered in the gall of bitterness and died months later. Her refusal to repent was all because of her pride. She could be alive today if she would not have allowed her pride to block the Holy Spirit.

Many believers today are blocking the Holy Ghost by operating in Pride and don't even realize it. One of the six things that Solomon says the Lord hates is a *"Proud look (Proverbs 6:17)."* In this new E.R.A., there is no room for Pride, only humility. There is only room for humility! It is through this vein that the Holy Spirit will function through God's remnant. Humility points to Jesus, while Pride points to self.

Pride says, "Look at me and what I have. Look at my car. Look at what my husband or wife did. Look at what my kids did. Look at how much money I have. The key word here is **my**,. Haylael's (Lucifer's) favorite words were, *I, Me, Myself, My, Mine.* In this age of social media, everyone is eager to showcase their stuff proudly. Pride displays the love we have for ourselves through boasting. It loves pleasure more than it loves God (2 Timothy 2:1-5). Look at where I've gone and who I've preached to. Look at how big my church is.

Look at my ministry. Pride is to ego what gasoline is to fire.

EGO:

Another deterrent to this new ERA and movement of the Holy Ghost is EGO. *E*, and *Go;* means everything must GO! I will never understand when ministers put their name in front of their ministries unless the Lord told them too. But if not then why? This is John Doe Ministries. It is not their ministry. It is the Lord's! Everything that will hinder us moving and living in this super-natural new ERA must be forfeited. The dictionary defines EGO as the self; An exaggerated sense of self-importance.

That self-importance can be critical because we want to believe that we had something to do with what God is doing in our ministries and our lives. Many ministers don't want to work with unknown ministers and sons of God, because they are jealous of the anointing on their lives. Also, they can sense the selflessness in their walk. If the Pastor does not see any monetary benefit in allowing these unknowns, they will block them the way they prevent the Holy Ghost with their EGO's. It's all about them. They say things like, *"Oh, My, Pastor so-and-so is really anointed.!"* And, *"Look at how accurately, that Prophet can hear from God!"* Comments like this laud the Pastor and swell his or her EGO. It makes their heads swell up as big as the

Jack-in-the-Box guy on the commercials. What would Moses attitude be?

Moses was more concerned about what the Lord's reputation was, then his own. *"Now if thou shalt kill all this people as one man, then the nations which have heard the fame of thee will speak, saying. (Numbers 14:15)"* In this new E.R.A., it is not about us. It's ALL ABOUT HIM! Even Jesus, Himself put away his ego. Paul writes, *"But made himself on no reputation, and took upon him the form of a servant, and was made in the likeness of men."* Are we willing to abandon other people's opinions of our appearance? We should only care about how we appear to Him. We must die to our EGO's by following Jesus and His commands.

We are to deny ourselves and take up the cross daily (Mark 8:34). In this new ERA, we must shed our EGO's and live for Him. What does Jesus want me to do? How does He want me to do it? Where does He want me to go? What does Jesus like? Our wills must no longer belong to us, and we are to be living sacrifices for the Master's use. Being void of self will enable The Lord God to use us in non-traditional ways.. Tradition will be an adversary in this new ERA.

TRADITION:

We are at a prophetic point in history; At the breaking of the dawn of a new age. Only God can lead us step by intricate step into this new E.R.A. that He has prepared for us. No living man has trodden down this path before. Only the Holy Spirit can lead us step by step in this new season. The pre-requisite is to flee from tradition.

I am going to make a prophetic statement: In this new E.R.A. we are not and have never been bound by the examples of Jesus Christ in the flesh before His resurrection, or the first twelve apostles or the New Testament Church or any Church in operation today. We serve an original God. Of course, we are to follow the principles of the examples that Christ left us. But tradition succeeds in binding you to the exact modes of Jesus and follow His examples in all things. That practice can't be done in this new E.R.A.

Our Lord Jesus Christ, in the days of His flesh, had no place to lay His head. Does that mean that I am to lie on the street if my loving, gracious, Heavenly Father in His infinite mercy has given me a place to stay? Shouldn't I be thankful and accept the blessings that he has provided for me? We are to follow Christ in the same faith, hope, and love. We are to emulate His nature, patience, wisdom and His vision. We should follow His relationship with The Father. We should empathize with His mercy and compassion for humanity. We should walk with the same Courage and in fighting sin, sorrow, and death. That's what we should exemplify.

If you try to follow the examples of the Apostles in this New E.R.A., you can't enter. Am I supposed to shave my head as Paul did at Cenchrae for his vow? For all those who are married, should you abandon your marriage because Paul wasn't married? Of course not. There are a lot of things that Paul and the Apostles did that I would not care to do just because of tradition. The point is that we are to be led by the Spirit in every aspect.

We are not supposed to gather around us twelve disciples, or our posse, because Jesus had twelve disciples. We also should not be working to get ourselves assassinated because He hung on a cross. If The Holy Spirit leads us to a Martyr's death, that is entirely different, but something that we must gladly do if required.

Tradition is a stronghold that blocks the **atomic** power of God. There is no need to attempt to duplicate precisely the way the early churches were structured or imitate the way their ministries functioned or operated. Being led by the Spirit means not caring how things have traditionally always been done. These old order forms and traditions of religious systems must be evacuated, immediately. It is not a way; It is life. It is not a method; It is the Spirit.

There are too many silly teachings among believers today, and all the ways have been tried in the past. Instead of relying on tradition, we should allow the Holy Ghost to bring forth in every assembly and congregation, the type of ministry that is suitable for that place and time. It will not always be the same way nor in the same form.

We can see by observing God's creation that He is a God of infinite variety. He is a manifold God. No two snowflakes are alike. Consider how different animals are. Tradition does not produce life. Children aren't even carbon copies of their parents. If they were, then you and your children should look, act, and think the same. Jesus never did the same thing the same way twice. When He healed blind Bartimaeus, Jesus merely spoke the word, "Go thy way, thy faith hath made thee whole," and he received his sight. When Jesus healed the two blind men in the house, He touched their eyes in addition to speaking a word. When He healed the man born blind from birth, He spat on the ground, made the clay of the spittle, and anointed the eyes of the blind man with the clay, and commanded him to wash in the pool of Siloam.

Many churches and fellowships today have been structured by the external manipulation of some misguided, self -appointed apostle or prophet. He supposes to have discovered God's move of the Spirit by imitating what God did two millenniums ago in a foreign and antiquated culture.

In this new E.R.A.; whatever we do, whatever we say, whatever we use, wherever we go, it MUST be by the Spirit. And the Holy Spirit is ORIGINAL; He is never stale or static. He is always fresh, new, and transcendental, and may never repeat what He did yesterday or the way He did it. The questions we should ask in this new E.R.A. are; What is God doing? How is He doing it? Is the actual presence of the Lord in this place? Is there the life of the Spirit in this place? We must live, move, and have our being in the Spirit, and get into His presence and let Him saturate us. We must open ourselves to be filled with the spirit of Jesus Christ and identify, locate, and die to SIN.

SIN:

Many churches and ministers do not preach about SIN. Most of the Bible lists sin and implores us not to engage in it. Who is the Bible written to? Believers. We

21

must repent daily and willfully turn away from conscious sin. In this new E.R.A. sin will keep you away from walking in the Atomic power of God as true sons and daughters of His kingdom. Even the sins that we do in secret and we think that no one is watching. Unfortunately, that's wrong; someone is always watching and always recording. You are never alone. Remember that! This new E.R.A, is a realm, a zone, or a kingdom, and there is no room for unrepentant sin in His kingdom.

Look at some of the lists of sins that Paul mentions that will prevent us from entering and operating in that **Nuclear** Power that Moses walks in. Paul writes, 9. *"Know ye not that the unrighteous shall not inherit the kingdom of God? Be not deceived: neither fornicators, nor idolaters, nor adulterers, nor effeminate, nor abusers of themselves with mankind. 10. Nor thieves, nor covetous, nor drunkards, nor revilers, nor extortioners, shall inherit the kingdom of God."(1 Corinthians 6:9,10).*

The word inherit is the Greek word *kleronomeo,* and it means to be an heir or sharer, and receive a heritage or a portion of the law of Moses and of the Gospel. When you receive your inheritance, then you can walk in this atomic, nuclear powerful realm of the kingdom. You can even recognize the word sin in *Sin*ai. A place where Moses was engulfed with the glory of God. Even Malachi tells us in Malachi 4:4, to *"Remember the law of Moses ..."* why? Because the law of Moses provides a guideline to sin-free living, to reach the Promised land of this new ERA; only if we rid ourselves of sin. We are told about sin to just put it away and not to do it.

So, there it is child of God. Get rid of your P.E.T.'S. Why? Because what lies before us is something that we've never seen before. In this new ERA, Pride, Ego, Tradition, and Sin will hinder and disqualify us. In this new ERA, it's the stuff that's beyond our wildest dreams. It is a new ERA, and what I can best describe as *T.N.H.B*. The Never Happened Before Realm, and it is labeled, ***Unprecedented: A New Thing***

Dr. Etienne M. Graves Jr.

Chapter III

Unprecedented: A New Thing

"Thou hast heard, see all this; and will ye not declare it?

I have shewed thee new things from this time, even

hidden things, and thou didst not know them."

• *Isaiah 48:6*

The Glory

On October 13, 2017, The Vision:

I was standing on a cliff-like type of mountain. All of a sudden, a prophet who looked like Moses, turned into a giant golden eagle. And the next thing you know I

25

was riding on the back of that Huge eagle. I had a rod (rod of Moses) on my back wrapped around my shoulder like a bow. There was a strong lightning type of bright light on the eagle that pulsated. It was similar to the scene in the movie, *"The Never- Ending Story."* In this scene, it's the end of the film and Bastian is riding on the back of Falkor the Luckdragon, with his hand raised in victory.

Do you see what I mean by Unprecedented? These types of things are unheard of in today's day and age, but The Lord is doing something new. One thing we know about Moses is that he was a miracle worker. In fact, he knew the Lord God by one of his seldom recognized monikers, *"Jehovah Mo-Faith."* The God of Miracles, Signs, and Wonders. Moses knew him personally. Did you know that Moses is the only prophet in the Bible called a *"god?"* *"And the Lord said unto Moses, See, I have made thee a* god *to Pharoah: and Aaron thy brother shall be thy prophet (Exodus 7:1)."* A lower case *g,* of course; but this should tell you the level of the power that he walked in and how close he was to *Jehovah Mo-Faith.*

Jehovah Mo-Faith dwells in the Un-precedented realm, and the things in this new ERA has no person on earth that can train us because there is NO PRECEDENCE! Well, who can teach us? The Holy Spirit, right? Of course, but there are many more tutors, teachers, and governors that are available to us in the Kingdom of the Lord Jesus.

"In these last days, the saints of old, those who have gone to glory, together with mighty angels in heaven are waiting to work together with us. We will need their help because there are many things that this

last days church- the remnant church is going to do for which we have no precedent. And we won't know how to do it, but these saints who have walked before us and are in glory now can help us along."- p.155, Sadhu Sundar Selvaraj, Last Days Seven Horns Anointing.

We must open our minds and spirits to the new thing that the Lord will do. If you don't think it is possible, look at Revelation 22:8,9. It states, 8. *"And I John saw these things and heard them. And when I had heard and seen, I fell down to worship before the feet of the angel which shewed me these things. 9. Then saith he unto me, See thou do it not: for I am thy fellowservant, and of thy brethren the prophets, and of them which keep the sayings of this book: worship God."*

A prophet came to show and teach John; not an angel. Can you see that some of these new things, that the Lord wants to do, really isn't new? But it is new to this generation because we have never seen it before. This new ERA must be decreed and declared before it manifests.*"Behold (look, pay attention), the former things are come to pass, and new things do I declare; Before they spring forth, I tell you of them."* (Isaiah 42:9). The word, declare is defined here as to announce (always by word of mouth), to expose, predict, explain, and manifest. To stand boldly out. Opposite. We are going to have to be holy and stand out from the world and wayward believers. We are not even supposed to remember or consider the old ERA or things (Isaiah 43:18).

The number eight means circumcision, cut off, curtail, put off, and new beginnings. It looks like two number zeros on top of each other. That's because you start over from zero. Observe some of these facts about the number eight in scripture. Isaac was circumcised after 8 days. Josiah became king at 8 years old (a new thing, never happened before). Jesus was not named until He was circumcised 8 days after He was born. The eighth chapter of the Bible is about Noah and his family, and the animals after the flood and their new beginning.

In *Colossians 2:11* we are told the prerequisite to enter into this new E.R.A. *"In whom also ye are circumcised with the circumcision made without hands in putting off (the old man) the body of the sins of the flesh by the circumcision of Christ."* We have to circumcise the sins of the flesh and our traditional way of thinking. God will never put anything new inside of something old.

The Word of God confirms this. 16. *"No man putteth a piece of new cloth unto an old garment, that which is put in to fill it up takes from the garment, and the rent is made worse. 17. Neither do men put new wine into old bottles: else the bottles break, and the wine runneth out, and the bottles perish: but they put new wine into new bottles, and both are preserved (Matthew 9:16,17)."*

As you can tell, circumcision is essential to God. God is not a respecter of persons and holds His word above all else. The Lord even held Moses accountable. God had given Moses the gift of the *"Miracle Anointing,"* but since Moses did not circumcise his son, according to the word of the Lord; which was symbolic of circumcision from sin, flesh, and traditional thinking, God was going to kill him. God wants us to move and have our being in this, *"Atomic Miracle Anointing,"* in this new ERA but we must be circumcised. In Exodus

4:24-26, we read, "*24. And it came to pass by the way in the inn, that the Lord met him (Moses) and sought to kill him (Moses). 25. Then Zipporah took a sharp stone, and cut off the foreskin of her son, and cast it at his feet, and said, Surely a bloody husband art thou to me. 26. So he let him go: then she said, A bloody husband thou art, because of the circumcision.*" We have to relinquish the old to wear the new.

The Lord loves new things. Don't you? When you wear a new pair of shoes, or drive a brand, new car, or purchase your own brand-new house, you feel good, confident, and excited. The Hebrew word for new is *chadash* and means fresh, to rebuild, renew, or repair. The Greek word for new is *neos* (Remember Neo from the Matrix movie). Neos means, new, youthful, and regenerate. The Lord says, "*Behold, I make all things new...*"

The ark of the covenant was set on a <u>new cart</u> (*2 Samuel 6:3*). Overcomers receive a <u>new name</u> *(Revelation 2:17)*. Jesus made a new and living way for us (Hebrews 10:20). Our covenant with Jesus is made new (*Hebrews 12:24*). The Bible mentions a <u>New Jerusalem</u>, a <u>New Heaven</u>, a <u>New Earth</u>, a <u>New Testament</u>, and <u>New Doctrine</u>. The Pharisees thought to heal and to cast out devils was a <u>new doctrine</u>. And it was; new to them. We are told to walk in newness of life (Romans 6:4). We are implored to put on the new man. We are invited to receive a spiritual makeover to restore us to a better condition. In the Anointed (Christ), we are all made into a new original creature (2 Corinthians 5:17). New beings operate in a new realm of an environment. One of these realms is the realm of *Infinity* where God dwells.

Eternity is where the supernatural atomic power of God, miracles, signs, and wonders, exist. In this new E.R.A, we will invade the realm of time through undaunted faith. The barrier between eternity and time will be so thin in this ERA, it will seem as though the veil between the natural and spirit worlds will be completely evaporated. Time was created by God on the fourth day. Faith is not created. Faith lies in a person; The person of Jesus Christ. This is unprecedented in the body of Christ. Unprecedented means never have done or known before. New. To God the words new and now are synonymous.

God is a Now God. Faith is always now. When were the new things in this new ERA created for us? The answer is, they weren't. God will create new things for us at the very moment that we need and ask for them, then he hides them in eternity until we can receive them, Now. Isaiah 48:6,7 states, *6. "I have shewed thee new things from this time, even hidden things, and thou didst not know them. 7. They are created now and not from the beginning..."* But how could you know this if no one told you the good news about it?

The gospel is good news or an announcement. News is new information of any kind. The doctrine of the kingdom is the good news or report about the realm, territory or zone of the atomic miracle power of the new ERA, and that Moses wore when I saw him. It's new! This gospel much be preached to the poor. The word poor in the Greek means to fail, fall, poverty, down, lack, no light upon. In the new E.R.A., this new thing once it touches your life will cause the poor to succeed, stand tall, have abundance, riches, and have the light of God shine upon them. The Lord has special messengers and supernatural assistants to accompany this new E.R.A. I call it the *Exciting Realm of Angels*.

Dr. Etienne M. Graves Jr.

Chapter IV

E.R.A. (Exciting Realm of Angels)

"Be not forgetful to entertain strangers: for thereby some

have entertained angels unawares (hidden)."

•   *Hebrews 13:2*

In a certain photo, right above my head, you can see a white orb or ball of light as I was worshipping The Lord God Almighty. This encounter goes to show an example of the many variations of angels that the Lord has at His disposal on our behalf. The Apostle Paul referred to these types of angels in Acts 20:8 when he raised Eutychus (good, well-fated) from the dead. 8. *"And there were many lights in the upper chamber, where they were gathered together."* In the verse before that, it states that it was midnight. So if these were natural lights, it would be evident that lights were on at that time. These are not natural lights, but angels.

On a warm, humid evening in Los Angeles, California, on around June of 1977, My Dad had an exciting, entertaining, terrifying, awesome, encounter. Being only about 5 or 6 years old at the time, I was in the room with my Mom and sister while my Dad was having a prayer meeting in the living room with a few of his friends. While he was on his knees, praying in the Spirit, a Seraph appeared and took him and his spirit out of his body up toward Heaven. As he looked back, he could see his body kneeling and still praying.

The creature that took him was a six-winged, huge, fiery Seraph. Can you imagine the awe and terror that must have gone through his mind? After being, snatched, taken, or grabbed, by the Seraph, they propelled upward. Up through the ceiling, through the night sky, past the stars, and planets to an astounding arrival in Heaven. Not just in Heaven, but before the throne of the Father God. The Father had all of these blessings behind him and told my Dad that if he would serve him, that he would give him all of those things. It seemed like a 3 D seen from Isaiah chapter 6. When the Mighty Seraph returned him to his body, he was weak for three days, and slept most of the time, until he recovered. It had such an indelible impact on him, and I did not know there would be some connection for my life with this encounter for my destiny even though I was only 5. What an exciting realm! Where angelic beings escort you to heaven. In the new E.R.A., these encounters will be widespread and occur often.

Well, precisely what is a Seraph? For that matter, many believers are ignorant of the identity of angels and how to work with them. According to the Bible, a Seraph means a burning, poisonous serpent, fiery, from their copper color; to be, cause, or set on fire. To cause to burn, or make to burn, kindle. The seraphim are angels of judgment. In Isaiah 4:4, Isaiah states, *"When the Lord shall have washed away all the filth of the daughters of Zion, and* shall *have purged the blood of Jerusalem from the midst thereof by the spirit of judgment, and by the spirit of burning."* The word burning has the same definition as the word Seraph. Before I go further in describing the role of seraphim, I want to explain their appearance.

Isaiah describes seraphim as having six wings. Two wings that cover their feet. Two wings that cover their face, and two for flying. They are huge with the appearance of a blow torch. Seraphim also speak. Isaiah heard them say, *"Holy, holy, holy, is the Lord of hosts: the whole earth is full of his glory* (Isaiah 6:3)." Their voice was so powerful that it caused the doors on the posts to shake, and because of the fire, the house was filled with smoke. Only Seraphim and Cherubim are mentioned as angels with wings in the Bible. I will discuss the Cherubim a little later in this chapter. In this new E.R.A., the Seraphim will be responsible for bringing the awareness of the supernatural kingdom of God toward His sons.

To make the sons aware of this spiritual kingdom, the seraphim will have to purge our DNA. In an instant, the spirit of burning that the seraphim bring forth can wipe clean the repetitive sins of our DNA. They will use the coals of fire to change the record of DNA, and bloodline. Devils look at our bloodline and read our DNA like a book. Demons lay it out like a map to find out our vulnerabilities.

The seraphim can eliminate and burn away these vulnerabilities with fire. That fire can burn away emotional problems and deep-rooted issues that can lead to counseling and therapy. This fire can deal with that in one minute. The fire can burn away memories, especially bad and harmful memories, especially those things that happened to us as children, that are affecting us as adults. Things such as hereditary problems, DNA deficiencies, addictions, habits, cycles, strongholds, bondages, and wrong mindsets. The fire of the seraphim does not just burn away the sins, but also the effects of the sin. The fire deals with the consequences of sin in our life. The devils that cling to us, oppress us and hang around us cannot stand the fire. The Cherubim have coals of fire between them, and their appearance is like burning coals of fire.

The cherubim have four wings and fly as do the seraphim. Except their appearance is different. They have four faces. The face of an ox, an eagle, a lion, and a man. They are awesomely dreadful in appearance. When the Lord placed Cherubim outside of the garden of Eden to protect the way of the tree of life. There was a flaming sword between them (Genesis 3:24). The Cherubim, similar to the seraphim bring the fiery judgment of God to be able to distribute God's mercy and scatter the coals of fire of repentance in this new E.R.A. His mercy is greater than His judgment. There are many different types of angels that have different roles and responsibilities.

Christ created all of the angels for our benefit. In Colossians 1:16, the Apostle Paul states, *"For by him (Christ) were all things created, that are in heaven, and in the earth, visible and invisible, whether they be thrones, or dominions, or principalities, or powers: all things were created by Him and for him."* Bless the Lord ye his angels that excel in strength, that do his commandments, hearkening unto the voice of his word (Psalms 103:20)." Don't forget his benefits. David proclaimed in Psalms, *"Blessed be the Lord, who daily loadeth us with benefits, even the God of our salvation, Selah."* In this new E.R.A., His angels are imposed with a heavy burden to treat and bestow on His children the service of goodwill as benefits to those who are saved.

Many don't believe in the service of angels because we have the Holy Spirit. However, in the book of Acts we can recognize the truth and the necessity of the work of both the angels and the Holy Spirit. Each has a separate role. The angels take orders from the Holy Spirit. *26. "And the angel of the Lord spake unto Phillip saying, Arise, and go toward the south unto the way that goeth down from Jerusalem unto Gaza, which is desert. 29. Then the Spirit said unto Phillip, Go near, and join thyself to this chariot (Acts 8:26,29)."*

Why couldn't the Holy Spirit tell Phillip to go to Gaza? It is because God's angels have a prevalent role in our lives and in this new E.R.A. The Greek definition of angels is the word *malak* which means messenger, to dispatch as a deputy (prophet, priest, teacher), king, employment, and occupation. We must not forget all of

Dr. Etienne M. Graves Jr.

His benefits, and one of them is the use of His angels. The point for us to grasp is there is a specific angel appointed for every assignment that God has given us! In the same fashion, angels are assigned to assist the Body of Christ in its collective and individual purposes from God on the earth. God releases these beings to minister, strengthen, and protect His children so that they may accomplish His work. Get the realization that in this new E.R.A., we are not involved in mere earthly endeavors: there is active warfare in the angelic realm. There is a real kingdom, animal kingdom, plant kingdom, human kingdom, and an angelic kingdom.

The Bible mentions many different types of angels. It says angels are strong, mighty, swift, elect, it numbers angels (12th, 7th, etc.). The Lord God mentions "mine" angel, The Angel of the Lord, and an Angel of the Lord. There are Seraphim, Cherubim, lights, wheels, eyes, Archangels, messenger angels, men in linen, thrones, dominions, powers, principalities, elements, winds, living creatures, beasts, hosts, ministering spirits, flames of fire, holy ones, warrior angels, watchers, and sons of God. The watcher angels and sons of God are special as they are the only angels with the ability to procreate and reproduce.

We must never forget that Jesus is so much better than the angels (Hebrews 1:4). Angels have personalities, intelligence, strength, emotions, and a free will. Angels have assignments and names. Angels have the power to choose, but not the right. Angels are immortal and created, not begotten of God by human DNA. Angels worship and are not to be worshipped. EVER! They are sent to protect and serve the saints, and sons of God, and

38

to facilitate God's precise movement in and around us. The angels accompany God's presence. In the new E.R.A., we are to cooperate with His holy angels, and not provoke them. Angels have done many things in scripture.

It is a seldom recognized fact that the law was given to Moses by angels. Look at Stephen's discourse in Acts 7:53, *"Who have received the law by the disposition of angels, and have not kept it."* Even Paul stated as much in Galatians 3:19, *"Wherefore then serveth the law? It was added because of transgressions, till the seed should come to whom the promise was made; and it was ordained by angels in the hand of a mediator."* Angels are very active in the Word of God.

God may very well have had an angel that looked like Him. He is called The Lord's Angel, or the Angel of the Lord. In Exodus 23:23. God tells Moses, *"For mine Angel shall go before thee...."* This Angel spoke as the Lord and acted as the Lord.

When Peter was freed from jail, the people didn't believe it because when Peter knocked on the door, they thought it was Peter's angel. Peter's angel seemed to have favored him as well because in Acts 12:15, 16, it is recorded, *"And they said unto her thou art mad. But she constantly affirmed that it was even so. Then said they, It is his angel. But Peter continued knocking: and when they had opened the door they were astonished."*

Even more astonishing is the ways that angels have been used to affect the material world. Angels baked a cake for Elijah, opened prison doors for the Apostles broke off the chains for Peter in prison by causing an earthquake, and burned with fire the bands of Shadrach,

Meshach, and Abednego. (1 Kings 19:5,6, Acts 5:19, 12:7, Daniel 3:25). An angel even stirred the waters at the pool of Bethesda (John 5:4). Theses angelic occurrences are exciting.

Holy Spirit announced that this new approaching E.R.A. is an acronym for Exciting Realm of Angels. The definition of the word exciting is causing great enthusiasm and eagerness. To produce a state of increased energy or activity in a physical system. To stir someone up and incite someone to do something. In this E.R.A. the many different types of angels will do things that have never been done before. EVER!

Chapter V

Living Creatures, Beasts, Hosts, & Men in Linen

*"And before the throne, there was a sea of glass like unto crystal: and in the midst of the throne, and round about the throne, were four **beasts** full of eyes before and behind."*

-Revelation 4:6

On the night of April 13, 2013, I received a text message from my favorite Aunt, Jocelyn Graves. Every time I would visit her she looked out for me and loved me as a son because I was her only nephew from her only brother. In the text, she said she was feeling anxiety and having trouble breathing. I texted her back and told her that I was about to call her and pray for her. She responded in another text and wrote that I did not have to call her, to pray for her. I immediately began praying for her. I then texted her one final time that I prayed for your instant healing and that the Holy Spirit would send his angels to minister to you and bless you in the mighty, matchless name of Jesus.

Unfortunately, the next afternoon, I received a phone call while I was at work that my Aunt was in the hospital on life support. I rushed out of my office and proceeded to the hospital in haste. As the family was in the waiting room in extreme sadness. I went to her and began praying in the spirit, in tongues for about 2 hours with tearful, violent force. I was oblivious to everyone who entered and exited the room, including doctors and nurses. I poured out everything within me to the Father God. I pleaded the blood of Jesus and His mercy in His name until exhaustion.

Well sadly, she passed away, the next day on April 15, 2013. Confused and bewildered, I wondered why my faith-filled intercession was not successful. I had never prayed like that before. At the Memorial service, in complete devastation still, I took a cell phone picture of one of the photos on display with her and I in it. Thinking nothing of it a couple of days later I was prompted to look at the picture that I took. I was amazed when I saw an eagle, or some fiery, heavenly beast or living creature with wings in the picture. In the picture it is very clear that you can see talons that appear to be grabbing me by my shoulders. In the original photo taken over 15 years before the memorial it does not appear. What was this creature in the photograph? From this, the Lord began to teach and show me about living creatures, beasts, hosts and men in linen. These entities will be a constant force for the people of God in this new E.R.A.

Living Creatures:

What exactly are living creatures and what does the Bible and the Holy Ghost have to say about them? Living creatures are not the best term for these creatures. Living beings is a better-suited label. The term "living creatures," is only mentioned in Genesis, Leviticus, and Ezekiel. In Strong's Concordance, *"living creatures,"* are defined as (chayah); alive, hence *raw* (flesh); fresh (plant, water, year), strong; also life or living thing, whether literal or figurative: + age, alive, appetite, (wild) beast, company, congregation, and springing troop. The term living creatures are only found in the Old Testament. Just like the many varieties of creatures there are in the natural world, there are just as many if not more in the spiritual world. It may be hard to fathom but the spiritual world is actually more real than the world we live in.

Beasts:

One of the different types of beings in the spiritual world is beasts. It seems like an expanded variation of living creatures that are described by John in the book of Revelation. But first let's examine the Hebrew word for beasts in the Old Testament, starting in Genesis. The Hebrew word for beasts is *bhemah*, (probably meaning to be mute), a dumb beast; especially any large quadruped or animal; the beast, or cattle. We can find this in Genesis

7:2, where it is stated, *"Of every clean beast thou shalt take to thee by the sevens, the male and his female: and of beast that are not clean by two the male and his female."*

So, we can conclude that there are spiritual animals just like there are in the natural. John mentioned the word beasts in Revelation 4:6-8. It is recorded, *"6. And before the throne there was a sea of glass like unto crystal: and in the midst of the throne, and round about the throne, were four beasts full of eyes before and behind. 7. And the first beast was like a lion, and the second beast like a calf and the third beast had a face as a man., and the fourth beast was like a flying eagle. 8. And the four beasts had each of them six wings about him, and they were full of eyes within: and they rest not day and night, saying, Holy, holy, holy, Lord God Almighty, which was, and is, and is to come."*

I find it interesting that one of the beasts had the face of a man, and even more perplexing that the beasts were called *"him."* The beast is like a man, and the man is like a beast. These four beasts are similar to the cherubim, except they only have one head each and are full of eyes before and behind. They are like the Seraphim in that they have six wings. One has a face like a lion, one like a calf, one like a man, and one like a flying eagle. And they also speak. Animals that speak?

The Greek word for a *beast* in this passage of scripture is *zoon,* and it means a live thing, an animal, beast that is alive and lives. It has the same meaning as *"living creature."* It is from this word that we get our words *zoo* and *zoology.* A zoo is a facility where living, typically wild animals are kept for public exhibition. The term wild animals are what stands out to me.

Hosts:

The word *hosts* are found only in the Old Testament, but we see it a lot. It is mentioned 286 times to be exact. We find it mentioned first in Exodus 12:41, as *"the hosts of the Lord."* The Hebrew meaning of the word *hosts* is *tsaba* and when it is broken down the meaning is powerful. It is defined as a mass of persons organized for war, engaging in a campaign for battle serving as soldiers. A massive army assembled to fight and perform in warfare. Every time hosts is mentioned it is a spiritual army ready to battle on behalf of the Lord and His children. He is called, Jehovah Sabaoth, "The Lord of Hosts." In Exodus 15:3, it proclaims, *"The Lord is a man of war: the Lord is His name."* He was the man that stood as *"The Captain of the host of the Lord,"* with His sword drawn in Joshua 5:14,15.

Men in Linen:

Both Ezekiel and Daniel speak of a man clothed in linen. This is not an ordinary man. One of these men were able to go in between the wheels of the Cherubim and take fire. This was no average man. He is like an angel. Men in linen are *"bad"* men. Not bad meaning bad, but bad meaning, not to be messed with.

The Hebrew word for linen here is *bad*. Listen to how Daniel describes the man in linen that he saw in Daniel 10:5-8. *"5. Then I lifted up mine eyes, and looked, and behold a certain man clothed in linen, whose loins were girded with fine gold of Uphaz: 6. His body also was like the beryl, and his face as the appearance of lightning, and his eyes as lamps of fire, and his arms and his feet like in colour to polished brass, and the voice of his words like the voice of a multitude. 7. And I Daniel, alone saw the vision: for the men that were with me saw not the vision; but a great quaking fell upon them, so that they fled to hide themselves. 8. Therefore I was left alone, and saw this great vision, and there remained no strength in me: for my comeliness was turned into corruption, and I retained no strength." The men in linen are no joke and powerful beyond imagination.*

They are like angels and appear as men and have spirit bodies. Contrarily not one Bible verse portrays angels as women or little fat, obese babies. They have feet, hands, eyes, faces, and physical appearances. They are supernatural beings that are immortal, powerful, mighty, exhibit great feats of strength, have tremendous speed, the ability to fly, and need no rest. They have volition, intelligence, and communicate.

In Genesis 18:2, it states three men, not angels appeared in the tent door. In Genesis chapter 19:3,10,16 we see that these men in linen ate food, rescued Lot bodily, shut his door and physically led his family out of the city. These men are like governors or lords who magistrate and rule at the command of The Lord. When we read of men in linen there follows supernatural occurrences for righteousness sake.

Men in linen have the power to destroy whole cities and unleash tremendous signs and wonders. They are usually clothed in white linen and glow and shine. I remember the time I saw one. He was in an all-white linen suit and he glowed and shined in a light whiter than bleach, and I was terrified.

In Zechariah 1:8-10, there were *men* whom the Lord had sent to walk to and fro on the earth. In Mark 16:5, it states, *"And entering the sepulcher, they saw a young man sitting on the right side, clothed in a long white garment and they were affrighted.* These men in linen bring a holy, terrifying, reverent fear when they appear.

In Luke 24: 2-5, we read, *"2. And they found the stone rolled away from the sepulchre. 3. And they entered in and found not the body of the Lord Jesus. 4. And it came to pass as they were much perplexed thereabout, two men stood by them in shining garments: 5. And as they were afraid, and bowed down their faces to the earth, they said unto them, why seek ye the living among the dead?"* These men in white linen bring revelation. Finally, In Acts 1:10 it says, *"And while they looked steadfastly towards heaven as he went up, behold, two men stood by them in white apparel."* In this New E.R.A., when God sends forth his angels, living creatures, beasts, hosts, and men in linen it will not be visible to the naked eye. Angelic activity goes on behind the scenes. It very well may be that activities will take place in human affairs for which man will not be able to account for or have an explanation.

Dr. Etienne M. Graves Jr.

Chapter VI

Wonder Men

"Here now, O Joshua the High Priest, thou and thy

*fellows that sit before thee: for they are **men wondered at***

for behold, I will bring forth my servant the BRANCH.:

Zechariah 3:8

In this new E.R.A. that we are about to embark on these *men wondered at* will come to help those of us on Earth who the Lord has predestined to walk in this unprecedented realm with unprecedented power. But who are these *men wondered at* that the Bible speaks of? First, let's define what this word *"wondered"* means?

The Hebrew meaning of this word is *mowpheth* and it is pronounced *mo-faith.* I believe it is because these men had more or should I say mo faith than ordinary men who walked the earth. It is defined as attracting obvious attention; a miracle; by a token or

49

omen, sign and wondered at. Also to be bright, and beautiful. They attracted attention because they had such an extraordinary measure of faith that they performed mighty miracles, signs, and wonders that they and their lives depict beauty beyond compare.

Before we delve into the place where these men dwell, let's discuss who they are? I know you have heard of wonder woman, but how about wonder men who were wonderworkers? These are the men mentioned in Hebrews chapters 11 and 12. They are the ACTUAL cloud of witnesses. We are told in Hebrews 12:1, *"Wherefore seeing we also are compassed about with so great a cloud of witnesses, let us lay aside every weight and the sin which doth so easily beset us, and let us run with patience the race that is set before us."*

We are surrounded by saints who act covertly and cheer us on as we run the race of life. We are like competitors being thwarted about with obstacles and stumbling blocks from every direction by our adversaries (the devil and his angels). It is a conflict, a fight, or a contest as we endeavor to accomplish that which the Lord has set before us. They root for us, but even more so in this new E.R.A., they will come to help us. They are cheering us on as if we are in an Amphitheater in a boxing or wrestling match.

In this race in the new E.R.A., we are like the anchor in a relay race and can't afford to drop the baton. They testate to our actions, are saddened by our failures and will rejoice in our victories. When we recognize them and understand their function and mandate on our lives, we will be able to cooperate with the ones he has assigned to us fully. To discover some of their identities, we must look in the previous chapter of Hebrews 12; chapter 11. This chapter mentions, Abel, Enoch, Noah, Abraham, Isaac, Jacob, Joseph, Moses, Rahab, Gideon, Barak, Samson, Jephthae, David, Samuel, and the prophets. These are the men wondered at. Later in the chapter entitled, *"Real Super(heroes),"* we will accentuate some of their exploits.

In the book of Matthew, we see them make their grand reappearance at the resurrection of our Lord and Savior Jesus Christ. Matthew 27:51-53, we are informed, *"51. And behold the veil of the temple was rent in twain from the top to the bottom; and the earth did quake, and the rocks rent; 52. And the graves were opened; and many bodies of the saints which slept arose, 53. And came out of the graves after his resurrection, and went into the holy city, and appeared unto many."* They returned and arose out of their graves, but we are never told that they went back to heaven with the Lord Jesus. Five hundred people witnessed only Jesus (one) return on a cloud into heaven.

We are not to pray to the men wondered at or the saints as some religions suggest. We are commanded to only pray to the Lord God, Our Heavenly Father who is in Heaven, but as I described what happened to me when Moses came, I did not pray to him or to God for him to come, He was sent. He came through a door that opened. So he and they were/is already here, hidden and ready to come to the ones that he and the men wondered at are assigned to go to in this new E.R.A.

Is there scriptural evidence of the men wondered at (saints or prophets) coming to men to bring revelation, assistance, and truth? The answer is yes! Observe what is said in Revelation 22:8,9, "*8. And I John saw these things, and heard them. And when I had heard and seen, I fell down to worship before the feet of the angel which shewed me these things. 9. Then saith he unto me, See thou do it not: for I am thy fellowservant, and of thy brethren the prophets, and of them which keep the sayings of this book: worship God.*"

The person who came to John was a prophet of the past and not an angel. However, John thought he was an angel. This tells you the glory and power that was surrounding this man and caused John to wonder at him like an angel. We are not to worship angels, spiritual beings, or prophets. As the scripture records, we are only to worship God! These men wondered at are now part of God's Divine Council and are included in The Father's decision-making process and involved in Divine discussions.

These men wondered at are what Hebrews 12:23 refers to as *"spirits of just men made perfect."* We are told in the book of Daniel, that the Watchers (certain angels) have the power to make decrees. This is the same authority that has been given to these men wondered at. There is an abundance of scriptural evidence that God works with an inner council of spirit beings to rule the affairs of creation.

Many verses are proving that God has a divine council, and these men wondered at are a part of this council. It is located in Job 1:6, 2:1, Isaiah 6:1-8, 42:9, Zechariah 3:7,8, Daniel 8:13-19, Hebrews 12:1, and Revelation 1:1, 22:7-9.

But the particular one that I would like to highlight is found in 1 Kings 22:19-23. *"19. And he said, Hear thou therefore the word of the Lord: I saw the Lord sitting on his throne, and all the host of heaven standing by him on his right hand and on his left. 20. And the Lord said, Who shall persuade Ahab, that he may go up and fall at Ramoth-gilead? And one said on this manner, and another said on that manner. 21. And there came forth a spirit, and stood before the Lord, and said I will persuade him. 22. And the Lord said unto him, Wherewith? And he said, I will go forth, and I will be a lying spirit in the mouth of all his prophets. And he said, Thou shalt persuade him, and prevail also: go forth and do so. 23. Now therefore, behold the Lord hath put a lying spirit in the mouth of all these thy prophets, and the Lord hath spoken evil concerning thee."*

Let us also not forget how the prophets Moses and Elijah appeared to the Lord Jesus on the Mount of Transfiguration in Matthew chapter 17. So even He received the assistance and counsel of men wondered at.

"Similarly, our relatives, forefathers, and those dear to our hearts who have died in Christ are sometimes sent by God to help us along our earthly journey. God sends them instead of angels because they can sympathize with us better, for they too lived in the world and experienced all kinds of trials, hardship, and predicaments. The scriptures testify: "For He Himself has suffered, being tempted, He is able to aid those who are tempted." (The Maharishi of Mt. Kailash, pgs. 33, 34, Sadhu Sundar Selvaraj).

There are many more *men wondered at* that I did not mention. I'm sure you would be surprised to know that many men who were involved in the Healing revival that swept across the world several decades ago, have gone on to glory and have become part of the Divine Council and qualified to be labeled, *men wondered at* as well. They will assist in the new E.R.A. where healing will be for ALL.

Chapter VII

He Healed Them ALL

"But when Jesus knew it, he withdrew himself from

thence: and great multitudes followed him, <u>and he healed</u>

them all;"

-Matthew 12:15

Have you ever been to or seen a healing crusade where everyone is healed? Probably not because those occurrences are rare and few and far between. There are trickles of people who are healed. It is almost like a lottery where some might receive their healing miracle while most don't. How can this be when most who attend, do so in expectation and anticipation of receiving their healing regardless of how dire their condition may be? Is it because they don't have as much faith as the small pockets of those who are healed? Or, how about the many hospitals, nursing homes, intensive care units, and mental institutions? These are those who can't make it to a crusade or church meeting to grab hold of their miracle of healing.

We are in the dawn of a new E.R.A where everyone who attends a church service or revival meeting will be healed. An E.R.A. where whole hospitals, I.C.U.'s, and mental institutions will be emptied out of their patients because a man or woman accompanied by the ministering spirits and angels of The Holy God will walk through with same fullness of the healing anointing that rested on Jesus Christ. When Jesus came on the scene almost anywhere everyone was healed!

We have a covenant with Jesus because of His precious blood he shed when He died for us on Calvary. Deuteronomy 5:2,3 states, *"2. The Lord God made a covenant (to render clear) with us in Horeb (destroy being devoid of comfort or hope). 3.The Lord made not this covenant with our fathers, but with us, even us, who are all of us here alive this day."* There is also another promise in Deuteronomy 7:15, that enunciates, *"And the Lord will take away from thee all sickness, and will put none of the evil diseases of Egypt, which thou knowest, upon thee, but will lay them upon all them that hate thee."* To the Lord diseases are evil, and Jesus came to destroy ALL evil and save them that are lost.

I want to highlight the plethora of times that the Lord Jesus healed ALL whom He encountered. When the Pharisees held a council against Him, guess what Jesus did? Matthew 12:15, records, *"But when Jesus knew it he*

56

withdrew himself from thence: and great multitudes followed him, and he healed them all."

How about in Matthew 4:23,24, *"23. And Jesus went about Galilee, teaching in their synagogues, and preaching the gospel of the kingdom, and <u>HEALING</u> all manner of sickness and all manner of diseases among the people. 24..."... And they brought unto him all sick people...... and he healed them..."* He healed everyone from whatever type of sickness and disease they were suffering from. It didn't matter what it was! If they were sick of ANYTHING, He healed them. In this new E.R.A., any type of ailment will be healed! All types of Cancer, Aids, Bubonic Plague, Ebola, Cholera, Diabetes, Pneumonia, Heart Disease; Whatever you can name or think of it WILL be healed in this new E.R.A. The angels will be used in this exciting fashion by Jesus.

Let's look at some more biblical evidence as Matthew 8:16 utters, *"When the even was come, they brought unto him many that were possessed with devils: and he cast out the spirits with his word, and healed all that were sick."* Isn't clear and evident that the Lord Jesus' intention is for <u>everyone</u> to be healed of <u>anything</u>!

There is more in Matthew 9:35, *"And Jesus went about all the cities and villages, teaching in their synagogues, and preaching the gospel of the kingdom, and healing <u>every</u> sickness and <u>every</u> disease among the people."*

Again, in Matthew chapter 10 verse 1 we read, *"And when he had called unto him his twelve disciples, he gave them power against unclean spirits, to cast them out, and to heal <u>all</u> manner of sickness and <u>all</u> manner of disease."* Can you see how many times the word *"<u>ALL</u>"*

is used? In the above verse, we see that not only did Jesus do it, but so did his disciples. Along with the anointing of the Holy Spirit and the exciting assistance of the angels.

Yet another example of the disciples healing all is found in the book of Acts chapter 5 verses 15 and 16. *"15. Insomuch that they brought forth the sick into the streets, and laid them on beds and couches, that at the least the shadow of Peter passing by might <u>overshadow</u>* (enveloped in a haze of brilliancy, preternatural*) some of them. 16. There came also a multitude out of the cities round about unto Jerusalem, bringing sick folks, and them which were vexed with unclean spirits: and they healed <u>every one</u>.* " Do you see that everyone was healed, All of the sick folks and even the people who were inflicted with sickness because of unclean spirits?

Another thing to be noticed is that the miracle was the healing by removing the ailment. But Jesus had the power based on His authority to replace the body part with a brand new and regenerated body part, that had been affected and damaged by the sickness or disease. It is referred to as being made <u>whole</u>. In Luke 17:19, it states, *"And He said unto them, Arise, go thy way: thy faith had made thee whole."* There is a difference between being healed and made whole. Matthew 14:36 informs us, *"And besought him that they might only touch the hem of his garment: and as many as touched were made perfectly whole."* The meaning for the word perfectly whole is the Greek word *diasozo.* It is where we get the word disease from and it means to save thoroughly, to cure, preserve, deliver, heal, to make whole and avoid reoccurrence.

Unfortunately, sin can be the root cause of many sicknesses and diseases. It is more than likely possible and right that the destruction and removal of sin can annihilate these sicknesses and diseases. That's why sometimes the Lord Jesus would forgive people of their sins and then they would be completely healed.

In the Bible the Lord is called a plethora of times Jehovah Rapha, which means, to mend by stitching, to cure, cause to heal, physician, repair, make whole, abate, cease, let alone, and to weaken. That is a title and one of His names and His character. He is the Lord who is healing, the healer, recreator, regenerating, mending, stitching, resurrected One. It is merely what He does and enjoys doing.

But on top of that, there is a name or a title where few know Him as. This title will be prevalent in the new E.R.A. He is also called Jehovah Raphashanah. It means and purports as the Lord who duplicates, transmutes, do, speak, or strike again, alter, double, given to change, diverse, repeat, return, do the second time. That indicates that if He did it once then He will do it again. If he healed anyone of anything before, He is obligated to do it again, and repeat it. He may not do it the same way, but it will yield the same results. When the word says that He healed all manner of sickness and diseases, that is our basis for whatever we may need healing of in this new E.R.A. An E.R.A. where whoever can be healed of whatever! There is NOTHING IMPOSSIBLE with Him. NOTHING!

In the new E.R.A., anything that is missing can be replaced. That means that anyone missing any body parts such as limbs, fingers, arms, hands, legs, arms, eyeballs, and internal organs (heart, lungs, kidneys, etc.), can have them restored, made whole and replaced. This is verified by the scriptures. Matthew 15:30, 31, confirms by stating, "*30. And great multitudes came unto him, having with them those that were lame, blind, dumb, maimed (no feet, hands, body parts), and many others, and cast them down at Jesus feet; and he healed them: 31. Insomuch that the multitude wondered, when they saw the dumb to speak, the maimed to be whole, the lame to walk and the blind to see: and they glorified the God of Israel.*"

The dawn of the new E.R.A. of healing and body part replacement is confirmed by Anna Roundtree in her book, The Heavens Opened on page 22. "*As we stepped from the building, we could see thousands of angel trainees sitting on the lawn in twos with one or two of the redeemed. They were in deep discussions. I looked up at the sign over the doorway of the building toward which we were walking. I could not read it before, but now much to my amazement, it appeared clearly: BODY PARTS.*"

We will be working with these angels in the new E.R.A. Anna explains more on page 23. "*The warehouse was large, as large as the auditorium we had just left and as white as a clean room at a research facility. It seemed unusually bright in the building, as though the contents were either preserved or incubated in light. "This building holds an inventory of available parts of the human body," Clara (An angel) said. There were bins upon bins of parts of all colors and sizes.*" (The Heavens Opened page 23, Anna Roundtree).

For the will of the Father to be accomplished on earth by healing all who desire it and replacing malfunctioned and missing body parts with regenerated ones, it will take real supernatural heroes to cooperate with the angels of the Lord in the new E.R.A.

Dr. Etienne M. Graves Jr.

Chapter VIII

Real Super *Natural* Heroes

"(Of whom the world was not worthy:)....-Hebrews

11:38 "......but the people that do know their God shall be

strong, and do mighty exploits."

-Daniel 11:32

Hollywood has done an excellent job of portraying heroes to an unsuspecting public. There are so many movies about heroes and titans, and supernatural power. When children and even adults see these movies, they want to emulate and be just like them. Everyone wants to have superpowers.

When I was younger, the favorites were Superman, Spiderman, Batman, Aquaman, Wonder Woman, and my personal preference was the Incredible Hulk. I remember asking my Mother to paint me green so I could dress up like the Incredible Hulk for Costume Day at Elementary School. Of course, she vehemently refused! Currently, some of the favorites are the X-Men, The Avengers, Thor, Captain America, and movies like Twilight and Harry Potter.

However, these are all fictional characters, and the abilities that we fiend for are not real. Or are they? You see it never dawned on me that these *"superheroes"* with extraordinary abilities were glorifying beings that once lived on the earth a long time ago. They were Nephilim, better known as giants. They are now identified as unclean spirits and devils without a body, but they still have superhuman abilities. The heroes and titans of today depicted in cinema are actually idols or gods that the people made sacrifices to. Deuteronomy 32:17 testifies, *"They sacrificed to devils, not to God; to gods whom they new not, to new gods that came newly up, whom your fathers feared not."*

These Nephilim had incredible abilities and had even mixed their DNA with humans and animals. But they got their abilities by being anointed by the Holy Ghost. Remember Lucifer is the Anointed Cherub. He never lost his anointing or abilities; they just became perverted. This is also the case with the Nephilim, giants, sons of God, gods, or devils. However, you want to label them. And when they mixed their DNA with humans and birthed children, the humans received supernatural abilities. Such as a man with ability of a spider (Spiderman), or a man with abilities of a bat (Batman).

This is confirmed by the scripture in Genesis 6:3,4, *"3. And the LORD said, My spirit shall not always <u>strive</u>*

(rule, judge {as umpire}, controller, plead the cause) *with man, for that he also is flesh: yet his days shall be an hundred and twenty years. 4There were* <u>giants</u> *(nephilim) in the earth in those days; and also after that, when the* <u>sons of God</u> *came in unto the daughters of men, and they bare children to them, the same became mighty (giborim, powerful, giant, warrior) men which were of old, (to veil, character, concealed, vanishing point, past or future)* <u>men of renown</u> *(famous).* The word mighty is the Hebrew word gibborim and is literally defined as heroes. They had superhuman strength because of the Holy Ghost (The Spirit of God). These are the characters that we have seen and read about in the DC and Marvel comics. They were even known to have the ability to fly.

Observe what is recorded in the Book of Giants, *"(After a journey through the heavens Mahway (Titan, Giant) sees Enoch and speaks to him of his request) Mahway mountd up in the air as if upon strong winds, using his hands like eagle's wings.... (Mahway) Flying here and there. Enoch came a second time to Mahway (after he, Enoch, had warned Mahway about flying too close to the Sun." (Book of Giants).* These beings had the ability to fly. It may sound far-fetched but these are some of the powers that will be on full display by The Holy Spirit in this new E.R.A. when necessary through the children of God. It is written in Hebrews 6:5, and is called the *"powers (miraculous mighty power, to be able or possible) of the world (era) to come."*

"God is going to reveal His awesome, mighty powers - hidden since creation.....Even the angels in Heaven have not seen such power of the Holy Spirit yet......We all assume that all the angels in Heaven have

65

seen God demonstrating His awesome power when He spoke the worlds into existence. "The powers displayed during creation," the angel said, "pale in comparison to what God is going to do in these last days." (Last Days Seven Horns Anointing, Sadhu Selvaraj, pg.11). There are modern-day examples of a sample of this power that was on display, even flying.

*"**St. Joseph of Cupertino** (1603-1663) is one of the saints who is best known for levitating during prayer. He was often carried away by God for some distance. In the records of his life, seventy of his levitations and flights are recorded.*

***St. Gerard Majella** (1726-1755) was often taken into remarkable levitations, often being moved by God for great distances. On one occasion, two of his companions watched him rise into the air and fly with the speed of a bird to a distance of almost a mile. After seeing this, they would often retell of this amazing event of which they had been witnesses.*

***Saint Martin de Porres** (1579-1639) He could fly through the air, as well as bi-locate. Reliable eyewitnesses have testified that Saint Martin de Porres had been seen doing missionary work in Asia and Mexico, even though he never left Lima, Peru.*

***Saint Francis Xavier** (1506-1552) The reason he was so successful in his efforts of evangelism is because he was reportedly able to be in multiple places at the same time. These bi-locations St. Francis experienced happened very frequently and were seen and documented by many eyewitnesses.*

***St. (Padre) Pio** (1887-1968) God graced Padre Pio with many extraordinary spiritual gifts. Among them,* *the gifts of healing, tongues, bi-location, working of miracles and the ability to see and work with angels. Despite the gifts, he never put the gifts before the giver and always remained humble concerning them."* (Translation By Faith, Dr. Bruce D. Allen and Michael Van Vlymen, pg. 13). So, you see it is possible. Even those powers we have seen on display in comics, television, and in movies by Superheroes and villains was accomplished by many men in the Bible.

We are all familiar with the famous opening from the Superman cartoon, television program, and movie. *Faster than a speeding bullet, More powerful than a locomotive, able to leap tall buildings in a single bound, It's a bird! It's a plane! It's Superman!* But did you know the Bible is filled with real Supermen, who were Real Super-Natural Heroes empowered by The Holy Spirit actually to perform these acts from the fictional Superman show. We know that the ultimate Superman (Jesus) performed astounding mind-boggling acts as THE Real Super-Natural Hero. But I will show you from scriptures others who displayed superpowers.

"....and he (Joshua)said in the sight of Israel, Sun stand thou still upon Gibeon, and thou Moon, ...and the sun stood still and the moon stayed ." – Joshua 10:12,13.

"...the axe head fell into the water. And the man of God said where fell it? And he shewed him the place and. And he cut down a stick, and cast it in thither; and the iron did swim." – 2Kings 6:6.

"....and Ahab rode (chariot, vehicle), and went to Jezreel. And the hand of the Lord was on Elijah, and he girded up his loins, and ran before Ahab to the entrance of Jezreel." - 1 Kings 18:45,46.

30."*...by my God have I <u>leaped over a wall</u>. 35.He teacheth my hands to war, so that a bow of steel <u>is broken in my hands</u>. " 2 Samuel 22:30,35.*

"And it shall come to pass, as soon as I am gone from thee, that the Spirit of the Lord shall carry thee whither I know not...." 1 Kings 18:12.

"...behold a young lion roared against him. 6. And the <u>Spirit</u> of the Lord came mightily upon him, and he rent as he would a kid,, and he had nothing in his hand...." Judges 14:5,6.

And he put forth the form of an hand, and took me by a lock of mine head,; and the spirit lifted me up (levitation) between the earth and the heaven...." Ezekiel 8:2.

"...when <u>Peter</u> was come out of the ship, <u>he walked on the water</u> to go to Jesus." Matt. 14:29.

"....the <u>Spirit of the Lord caught away</u> Phillip, that the Eunuch <u>saw him no more</u>...."Acts 8:39.

And when Paul had gathered a bundle of sticks and laid them on the fire, there came a <u>viper</u> out of the heat and fastened on his hand. 5. And he shook of the beast into the fire and <u>felt no harm</u>. 6,Howbeit they looked and when he should have swollen or fallen down dead suddenly: but after they looked a great while, and <u>saw no harm</u> come to him, they changed their minds and said that <u>he is a god.</u>" Acts 28:3-7.

These Real heroes did everything that was mentioned in the Superman intro and so much more. And it was real, and occurred. There is only one way that this happened and will happen. *"....Not by <u>might</u>, nor by power, but by my Spirit, saith the Lord of <u>hosts</u>." Zechariah 4:6.* It won't be by might or by power but by

The Holy Spirit. In this new E.R.A., God will use ordinary men and women to perform extraordinary acts that we can't even fathom. In this new E.R.A. that we are embarking on we will see and do things that we have NEVER done before, and it is all because of the ultimate Real Super-Natural Hero, called *"Neverman,"* and He will come to the rescue.

Dr. Etienne M. Graves Jr.

Chapter IX

Neverman to the Rescue

*"The officers answered, **Never man** spake like this man."John 7:46*

This new E.R.A. will be the dimension of the never happened before. A dimension beyond mere sound, and sight, and mind. It will be an E.R.A. beyond shadow and the substance of things hoped for. It is the E.R.A. and dimension of the Now zone. In the now zone everything is new because it has not been seen before. *Eye has not seen nor ear heard, neither have entered into the heart of man, the things (New things) which God has prepared for them that love Him." 1 Corinthians 2:9.*

The Lord will use His angels to herald this new E.R.A. Isaiah 43:18,19 proclaims, *"18. Remember ye not*

71

the former things, neither consider the things of old.19. Behold I will do <u>a new thing (fresh, repair, renew)</u>; <u>now</u> it shall spring forth; shall ye not know it? I will even make a way in the wilderness, and rivers in the desert." God is known for doing new things, and things never were done before. Did you know that before the flood and God's announcement to Noah, it had <u>never</u> rained before? Genesis 2:5 verifies this, *"....for the Lord God had <u>not</u> caused it to rain upon the earth.*

I want to point out some revelation about the number eight, to display how much the Lord loves new beginnings and doing unusual things, and He will use His angels in exciting ways to do so. The number 8 represents new beginnings. He put the man in the garden on the eighth day.

Genesis chapter 8 represents a <u>new</u> world with <u>new</u> beginnings after the flood. After eight days the male child was to be circumcised and therefore constituted a new start. Genesis shows us only eight people survived the flood to begin the new E.R.A. I Peter 3:20, informs us, that only eight souls were saved by water.

As I mentioned before, Jesus was not named until after His circumcision, eight days later. Luke 2:21 confirms, *"And when eight days were accomplished for the circumcising of the child, his name was called JESUS, which was so named of the angel before he was conceived in the womb."*

Remember, Josiah became king at eight years old, and that had never happened before. The word or number eight is in the Bible eighty times. We will see unique and exciting new things in this new E.R.A. because the Heavenly Father's Holy Angels will be busy and at work.

People who need help, assistance and guidance from God will receive it from Never man.

Who is Neverman? Jesus is Neverman. He will come to our rescue and do things for us that we could have never expected. He is the head of the angels. When the angel went down to stir the waters at the pool of Siloam, there was a man, who had *never* been able to see. But when Neverman (Jesus) stepped on the scene, he was healed and received what He had never had before. Sight! In the new E.R.A. Neverman will make things happen that has never happened before.

Even Matthew recorded it in Matthew 9:33, when he wrote, " *And when the <u>devil was cast</u> out, the dumb spake: and the multitudes marvelled, saying, "It was <u>never (special), so seen</u> in Israel.* " Forget Marvel comics, the people marveled because they had never seen anything so special. That's what going to happen in this New E.R.A. People will see things so special that they will be stuck in awesome wonder. And it will all be because of Jesus, the real Super Hero; Neverman. The Bible even calls Him Neverman.

"Now in the place where He was crucified there was a garden; and in the garden a new <u>sepulchre</u>, wherein was <u>NEVER Man</u> yet laid." (John19:41). "And he took it (Jesus' body) down, and wrapped it in linen, and laid it in a sepulchre (remembrance) that was hewn in stone, where NEVER Man before was laid." (Luke 23:53). When they asked the question, "What manner of man is this, that even the winds and the sea obey Him? The answer is Neverman!

In this new E.R.A. Neverman will operate through the mature sons of God. The Bible does not record everything that Jesus did. Therefore, the exploits that will be done through us will be unprecedented. John 20:30, 31 tells us, "*30. "And many other signs truly did Jesus in the presence of His disciples, which are not written in this book:31. But these are written that ye might believe that Jesus is the Christ..."*

The dawn of this new E.R.A. is going to be accompanied by new things because our Heavenly Father has always done new things. Matthew 9:16, 17 proclaims, "*16. "No man putteth a piece of new cloth unto an old garment, that which is put in to fill it up takes from the garment, and the rent is made worse. 17. Neither do men put new wine into old bottles: else the bottles break, and the wine runneth out, and the bottles perish: but they put new wine into new bottles and both are preserved."*

Neverman (Jesus) makes all things *new*. There will be a *New* Jerusalem, a *New* Heaven, and a *New* Earth. There is a *New* Testament, and we walk in *New*ness of life. (Romans 6:4). The Apostle Paul tells us to put on the *new* man. (Ephesians 4:24, Colossians 3:10). The new man is Christ Jesus also referred to as *Neverman*.

Second Corinthians 5:17 says, *"If any man be in Christ, he is a new creature.: Behold all things are become new."* Jesus came and commissioned us to preach the gospel of the kingdom to every creature.

The word gospel is the Greek word euaggelizo which means to announce good *news* (evangelize) especially the gospel: declare, bring glad tidings. It is a combination of two words: good and angel or messenger. An angel brings the good news of the kingdom. The good news is that whatever you've never had before, or never been able to do; it can be done and received in this new E.R.A. (Exciting Realm of Angels) through Neverman (Jesus). The news is new information of any kind, including new things.

The good news to a person who has always lacked is that in the new E.R.A. he never has to lack again in Christ. The gospel is the good news that you can have what you've never had through Neverman. The age of being unable, impossibility, and impotence are coming to close. In this E.R.A. that is closing, there is so much turmoil, misunderstanding, and fear that I have been commissioned to proclaim and declare that a new E.R.A. approaches. One that will open your eyes to the hope of life and life more abundantly.

Look at what it says in Acts 14:7-11, "*7. And there they preached the gospel (announce good news). 8. And there sat a certain man at Lystra (that which dissolves or disperses), impotent (impossibility) in his feet, being a cripple from his mother's womb, who had NEVER walked: 9. The same heard Paul speak: who steadfastly beholding him, and perceiving that he had faith to be healed, 10. Said with a loud voice, Stand upright on thy feet. And he leaped and walked.*"

Paul was clothed with the new man. Who is the new man? Neverman or Christ. When Never-man steps on the scene impossibilities become possibilities, Neverman is the complete embodiment of the new creature. A New CREATURE *(original formation, creation)* in Christ – A New Man for a New Age. "*.....for to make in Himself of twain one new man....*" –Eph. 2:15. "and have *put on(array, sink into) the new man,* which is *renewed* in *knowledge*, after the *image of him that created (formed) him."* Colossians 3:10.

It is because of His love for us that we are baptized into the realm of the Neverman to become anointed, covered, and enabled to move into His liquid love anointment oil. *"For as many of you have been (were) baptized (cover over) into Christ (the anointed) have put on Christ." –Gal.3:27, Rom. 3:14.*

Chapter X

Liquid Love Anointment Oil

"And it shall come to pass in the last days, saith God, I

will pour out my Spirit upon all flesh: and your sons and

daughters shall prophesy, and your young men shall see

visions, and your old men shall dream dreams: And on

my servants and on my handmaidens I will pour out in

those days of my Spirit; and they shall prophesy:"

Acts 2:17,18

In Hebrew the word pour is *shaphak,* and it means to spill forth blood, libation, a liquid, to pay out life, money, a pipe for pouring forth, and gush out. In the new

E.R.A. He will pour out His Spirit in a spiritual liquid form. If something is poured out, it will be in liquid form. God will use His Holy Angels to pour out His liquid love upon us. This liquid love is supernatural in every way.

In ceramics to shape and form figures the clay has to be wet. Look at Jeremiah 18:3-6, "*3. Then I went down to the potter's house, and, behold he wrought a work on the wheels, 4.. And the vessel that he made of clay was marred in the hand of the potter: so he made it again another vessel, as seemed good to the potter to make it ....6. O, house of Israel cannot I do with you as this potter....as the clay is in the potter's hand, so are ye in mine hand.*" - Jer. 18:3-6. In the new E.R.A., everything and everyone that is marred can be made new. It is because of His love for mankind.

There is nothing more powerful than the love of God. Song of Solomon 2:4, states, "*He brought me to the banqueting house, and his banner over me was love.*" A banner is a raised standard or flag that is flaunted. Before Adam and Eve were expelled from the garden of Eden, the Bible says they, "were not ashamed." The definition of the word ashamed is to become dry. They felt God's liquid love and were soaking wet with it.

The recognition of God's love removes shame, guilt, embarrassment, unworthiness, disgrace and dishonor of condemnation. When we can cling to His love, it will hold back and restrain the darkness, the misery, the sadness, uncertainty, confusion and attachment to shame. Christ's agape love enables Him to love us and us to be loved by Him. Song of Solomon 8:6,7 states, "*6. Set me as a seal upon thine heart, as a seal upon thine arm: for love is as strong as death;*

jealousy is cruel as the grave: the coals thereof are coals of fire, which hath a most vehement flame. 7. Many waters cannot quench love, neither can floods drown it: if a man would give all the substance of his house for love, it would be utterly contemned." Jesus' love is unmatched.

In John 15:13, the Bible tells us the credentials for the greatest love of all, and it is not Whitney Houston's definition. In the book of John, it proclaims, *"Greater love hath no man than this, that a man lay down his life for his friends."* Jesus laid down His life for us and called us His friends. There is no greater love than the liquid form of His precious, powerful, wonder-working blood (liquid love). In the new E.R.A., it will be abundantly dispersed and poured out, *"by the Holy Ghost, by love unfeigned (not hypocritical)." (2 Corinthians 6:6).*

The Lord's cry to the church of Ephesus, in Revelation 2:4, is that they have left their first love. The liquid love anointment oil brings real emotion and feeling. When you love someone, it is accompanied by genuine feelings and emotions. When Jesus had heard that his friend Lazarus had died, He began to weep. Look at John 11:34-36, *"34. And said, Where have ye laid him? They said unto him, Lord, come and see. 35. Jesus wept. 36. Then said the Jews, Behold how <u>he loved him!</u>"* Love is a decision of power backed up by action. Of course, Jesus went on to raise Lazarus from the dead.

In Psalms 63:1-3, His glory and power are connected to His lovingkindness. Please notice that the two words, loving and kindness are combined to make a compound word. Because He is loving, His kindness follows right behind a display of that love, that is poured out as a liquid like water. The scripture in Psalms 63 reads, *"1. O God, thou art my God; early will I seek thee: my soul thirsteth for thee, my flesh longeth for thee in a dry and thirsty land, where no water (liquid love) is. 2. To see thy power and thy glory, so as I have seen thee in the sanctuary. 3. Because thy loving-kindness is better than life, my lips shall praise thee."*

The word lovingkindness is the Hebrew word *Checed,* and it means beauty, favor, kind and good deeds, mercy, reproof, to bend or stoop and show mercy and kindness to an inferior, pity on and grant grace. The psalmist says it is better than life itself. This liquid love anointment oil of loving-kindness will distinguish as and show the marvelous wonder of the Holy Spirit.

He loves us unconditionally, but He will not justify or accept our lifestyle if it does not line up with the principles and scripture of God (sin). Nothing can separate us from the love of Christ, and the love of God which is in the Anointed Jesus our Lord. (Romans 8:35-39).

The anointing on David was that the fact that his name means beloved. He knew that God loved him and that empowered him through his faith in God to defeat Goliath. Jesus was rejected on the cross so that you and I can become His beloved. Ephesians 1:6 tells us, *"To the praise of the glory of his grace, wherein he hath made us accepted in the beloved."* When Jesus was baptized in liquid in Matthew 3:16, 17, The Father spoke from Heaven, and said, *"This is my beloved Son, in whom I am well pleased."* The Father even personalized it in Mark 1:11, *"And there came a voice from heaven saying, Thou art my* beloved Son, in whom I am well pleased." It was changed from this is to thou art.

In the next two verses in Mark chapter one, Jesus was driven to the wilderness by the Holy Spirit to be tempted by Satan. It was essential for him to to know that He was loved. This statement was so powerful that when Devil came to tempt Jesus in the wilderness, that Satan purposely omitted this when he addressed Jesus. In Matthew 4:6, Satan addressed him in this way, *"If thou be the Son of God.."* But He wasn't just the Son of God, and He was the *Beloved* Son of God. Satan did not want Jesus to be reminded of the Father's love for Him because it is therein that the realization that Satan is more than defeated and rendered powerless. *"Beloved, let us love one another: for love is of God; ....God is love."* (1 John 4:7,8). We will be dripping or better yet thoroughly drenched with the liquid love anointment oil in this new E.R.A.

It is like the cloud of His glory. A cloud is a visible mass of particles of the condensed vapor such as water suspended in the atmosphere of a planet. In Genesis 2:6, a mist went up from the Earth and watered the whole ground with the liquid love anointment oil.*''....our fathers were under the cloud (to cover over, practice magic) and all passed through the sea; 2. And were all baptized (to cover wholly in a fluid) unto Moses (draw out of the water, rescue) in the cloud and in the sea; 3. And did eat the same spiritual meat; 4. And did all drink the same spiritual drink: for they drank of that spiritual rock that followed them: and that Rock was Christ." 1 Corinthians 10:1-4.*

The Hebrew word for cloud is *anan,* and it means the nimbus or thunder cloud, a rain cloud, to cloud over, act covertly, practice magic, observer of times.

Can you see the power of the liquid love anointment oil in this new E.R.A.? In the Harry Potter movies, he rode a magic broomstick named *Nimbus 2000.* We just read the definition of cloud in the Hebrew. In the new E.R.A., Satan will try to counter the miracles and power of God just like the Egyptian magicians did against Moses in the book of Exodus. Satan decided to go ahead of this move of God coming in the new E.R.A. with the ice bucket movement several years ago, where everyone wanted to baptize themselves with ice water merely because they saw someone else do it. They didn't even understand the spiritual significance of it. It is countered by those who follow new age doctrine and the age of Aquarius.

The world looks to astrology and horoscopes (scopes of horror) for their guidance. But on the other hand the Bible does mention the zodiac in Job 38:32, *"...canst thou bring forth the <u>Mazzaroth</u> (Zodiac, constellations) in his <u>season</u> (time, now, adorn)."* Psalms 19:1-3 declares, *"1.The heavens declare the glory of GOD; and the firmament sheweth His handywork. 2. Day unto day uttereth speech, And night unto night sheweth knowledge. 3. There is no speech or language where their voice is not heard."*

What is it that the heavens are declaring about the new E.R.A. and the liquid love anointment oil? Aquarius is a constellation of the Zodiac depicting a man <u>pouring out a large urn of water</u>. Better known as a water carrier. An era begins a new date in the history and person of that thing. I have felt this liquid love anointment oil, and it is difficult to describe.

One day while praying in the spirit my hands began to tremble like a shaking leaf or like when paint is shaken to mix at tremendous speed, and in between my hands I could tangibly feel what felt like an oily, silky, smooth, greasy, and soft wind that left no residue but felt thin and light and slippery. I was told that it was the liquid love anointment oil that would be dispersed in the new E.R.A. Angels would be bringing it at the command of the Holy Spirit and pour it out as a liquid upon the armies and designated children of The Lord God Most High.

An ointment is a fragrant, rich, greasy, liquid that shines and is rubbed on the skin for medicinal or cosmetic purposes. This liquid love anointment oil combines the love of God with the anointing and ointment that will be poured out on all flesh. The angels will pour it out, and it will yield unprecedented, miracles, results that we could have never even imagined. God has anointment oil and His very own pharmacy that He created in the Garden of Eden that will become a prevalent way of living in the new E.R.A

Dr. Etienne M. Graves Jr.

Chapter XI

God's Amazing Pharmacy

"In the midst of the street of it, and on either side of the

river, was there the tree of life, which bare twelve

manner of fruits, and yielded her fruit every month: and

the leaves of the tree were for the healing of the nations."

•   *Revelation 22:2*

God cares so much about His children that He
planted a whole garden in Eden. A garden is a fenced in
protected area where herbs, fruits and flowers, and
vegetables are cultivated. It should be no surprise or
wonder that when Mary Magdalene saw Jesus after He
was resurrected, she thought Jesus was the gardener.

85

John 20:15 states, *"Jesus saith unto her, Woman why weepest thou? Whom seekest thou? She, supposing him to be the gardener, saith unto him, Sir, if thou have borne him hence, tell me where thou hast laid him, and I will take him away."* Have you ever wondered why of all things she thought He was the gardener?

It is in the garden where He put everything that we need to be healthy, happy, and whole. John tells us in Third John 1:2, *"Beloved (there's that word again), I wish above all things that thou mayest prosper and be in good health, even as thy soul prospereth."* In the new E.R.A., it is so imperative that we function in good health, that John informs us that he wishes that above all things for us.

Before the flood, our diet consisted of fruits, vegetables, and herbs. God placed a pharmacy in His garden. Any part of our body that may need healing, to be cured or strengthened is available in full supply in His garden. The chemicals, vaccines, and medicines offered to us in the world are full of side-effects, and never cure the ailment. Not to mention the G.M.O.'s (Genetically Modified Organisms), that lead to damaging our vessels and subtle poisoning that leads to an early death through diseases. In God's Amazing Pharmacy the fruits and vegetables look like and are shaped the same way as the body parts that they help are. They are clues to our health.

It's been said that God first separated the salt water from the fresh, made dry land, planted a garden, made animals and fish. All before making a human. He made and provided what we'd need before we were born, including a medical pharmacy. These are best and more powerful when eaten raw.

Walnuts:

Doesn't the walnut look like the brain? When it is opened it has what looks like the left and the right hemisphere. There are also parts that look like the left and the right cerebrums. There are even wrinkles like the neo-cortex! The amazing part is that the walnut is the best drug for the brain. Eating walnuts will help your brain develop a better brain function because they boost the neuron- transmitters by more than three dozen! The FDA is against the advertisement of the walnut as a cure because according to them only pharmacies do that.

Walnuts increase the omega-3 fatty acids in red blood cells and decrease total cholesterol. And they have incredible cancer-fighting properties.

Olives:

It is from olives that olive oil is made and used as an ingredient in the recipe for the anointment oil in the bible and used to anoint in the body of Christ today. Olives are known to assist the function of the ovaries, and overall health and look like them. According to an Italian study, women that eat more olives have 30% less chance of getting ovarian cancer. Olives are a great source of vitamin E and serve as a powerful vitamin in eliminating free radicals responsible for cancer cell formation through oxidation.

Regular consumption of extra virgin olive oil reduces the risk of getting colon cancer.

Carrots:

A sliced carrot looks exactly like the human eye. The pupil, iris, and radiating lines look just like the human eye. Medical science shows and proves that carrots greatly enhance blood flow to the eyes and function of them. It is known to improve our vision significantly.

Tomatoes:

A Tomato has four chambers and is red. The heart has four chambers and is red. All of the research shows tomatoes are loaded with lycopine and are indeed pure heart and blood food. Lycopine helps in type 2 diabetes and lowers cholesterol levels. It very much resembles a heart when cut in half. It helps in cleaning plaques from our coronary arteries that could rupture and cause heart attacks.

Grapes:

Grapes hang in a cluster that has the shape of the heart. Each grape looks like a blood cell and all of the research today shows grapes are also profound heart and blood vitalizing food. They contain polyphenols, powerful anti-oxidants which slow down or prevent colon, prostate, pancreatic, endometrial, pharynx, mouth, lung and esophageal cancer. The red wine made from grapes is also magnificent in improving the health of our heart.

Kidney Beans:

Kidney Beans heal and help maintain kidney function and yes, they look exactly like the human kidneys. The liquid in which you boil kidney beans can be used to melt kidney stones. Kidney beans are an excellent source of iron, fiber, they lower the risk of heart attack, stabilize the blood sugar, maintain your memory thanks to thiamin levels.

Celery, Bok Choy, and Rhubarb:

Celery, Bok Choy, Rhubarb and many more look just like bones. These foods specifically target bone strength. Bones are 23% sodium and these foods are 23% sodium. If you don't have enough sodium in your diet, the body pulls it from the bones, thus making them weak. These foods replenish the skeletal needs of the body. With just one celery stick you can aid in the weight loss process, reduce inflammation, relax, regulate your body's alkaline levels, aid digestion, improve your sight, reduce bad cholesterol and lower blood pressure.

Avocadoes, Eggplants, and Pears:

Avocadoes, Eggplant and Pears target the health and function of the womb and cervix of the female - they look just like these organs. Today's research shows that when a woman eats one avocado a week, it balances hormones, sheds unwanted birth weight and prevents cervical cancers. And how profound is this? It takes exactly nine (9) months to grow an avocado from blossom to ripened fruit. There are over 14,000 photolytic chemical constituents of nutrition in each one of these foods (modern science has only studied and named about 141 of them).

Onions and Garlic:

Onions look like the body's cells. Today's research shows onions help clear waste materials from all of the body cells. They even produce tears which wash the epithelial layers of the eyes. A working companion, Garlic, also helps eliminate waste materials and dangerous free radicals from the body. The Israelites of the Bible mentioned onions and garlic as a delicacy that they missed when they left Egypt. Onions help in the blood sugar regulation as well, thanks to the chromium. For centuries this amazing vegetable has been used to heal infections and reduce inflammation.

Figs:

Figs are full of seeds and hang in twos when they grow. Figs increase the mobility of male sperm and increase the numbers of Sperm as well to overcome male sterility. If you read my last book, *"Unveiling Secrets From Eden's Garden,"* then you would not be surprised why Adam and Eve covered themselves with fig leaves after they sinned in the garden.

Sweet Potatoes:

Sweet Potatoes look like the pancreas and actually balance the glycemic index of diabetics. Sweet potatoes are also an excellent source of vitamin A as beta carotene. They are great for dietary fiber and potassium.

Oranges, Grapefruits and Citrus Fruits:

Oranges, Grapefruits, and other Citrus fruits look just like the mammary glands of the female and actually assist the health of the breasts and the movement of lymph in and out of the breasts. Oranges also contain a high amount of vitamin C that can help the body recover from the flu.

Peaches:

Peaches look like the gluteus maximus or buttocks. They prevent constipation, Combats cancer, Helps stop strokes, Aids digestion, Helps hemorrhoids.

Wheat Germ:

Wheat germ is shaped like the colon and combats colon cancer, prevents constipation, lowers cholesterol, helps stop strokes and improves digestion.

In the new E.R.A., we will have to maintain our bodies in health to be able to sustain the power that God wants to release. The new E.R.A. will be exciting and unbelievable because we will experience the fire of

God's kingdom. It will be delivered by His angels. They will bring The fire of the God; who is a consuming fire because He makes His angels spirits and His ministers a flame of fire. In the new E.R.A., the fire of God will be poured out and dispensed by His holy angels. Many times when I lay hands on someone to pray for them, they tell me that they feel this heat emanating from my hands. It is the anointing of the Lord and the ministry of the exciting realm of angels. In the new E.R.A. flames of the fire of God will be more prevalent and widespread

Prayer/Decree for the Release of God's Holy Angels

In the name of Jesus, I am a citizen of the kingdom of Heaven, and I have access to all of the benefits of my salvation, including the Ministry of Angels. My Heavenly Father sends angels to serve me, work for me, and minister to me. I loose legions of angels to bring the answers to my prayers as they are sent by my Father in Heaven to me. I decree a release of Holy Angels of the Lord to encamp around about my family and me to protect us and our possessions.

Today Angels are loosed to shield and protect me from danger, harm, injury, accidents, catastrophes, and surprise attacks from the enemy in Jesus' name. I release the Angels of the Lord to reap and bring in my harvest as I confess the promises of the Word of God by faith. My Father has sent them to make a way where there is no way, and to make the impossible POSSIBLE.

Today Angels, the flames of fire fight for me in the heavenlies. I decree that Angels are released to supernaturally intervene in my life and every situation and circumstance that involves my family and me at the command of God. I loose my assigned angels to bring favor, provision, healing, deliverance, ideas, and blessings to me now in Jesus' name!

My Gracious Heavenly Father has sent His Holy Angels ahead of me to prepare my way. I decree a release of the Holy Angels to remove every stumbling block out of my life when necessary and to set up roadblocks when needed. The Chariots of the Lord are the fiery angels sent to defend me and my family. I loose the Heavenly Angels to aide in releasing me from debt and lack and to replace it with the supernatural, exponential and abundant provision.

I release the angels, and hosts of Heaven to fight for me and be victorious in bringing the Lord's purpose into my life. I decree and confess that my Saviour Jesus confesses me before the Father in Heaven and His Holy Angels. He has given His angels charge over me and works wonders for me daily in Jesus' (Yeshua's) mighty matchless name. It is DONE NOW! SO BE IT! GO, ANGELS

Works Cited

1. Graves Jr, Etienne M. *Demons Nephilim Angels: The World That Then Was.* Los Angeles: Trafford Publishing, 2014

2. Strong, James. *The New Strong's Exhaustive Concordance of the Bible.* Nashville: Thomas Nelson Publishers, 2010.

3. *The Companion Bible King James Version.* Grand Rapids: Kregel Publications, 1922.

4. Graves Jr, Etienne M. *Unveiling Secrets From Eden's Garden.* Los Angeles: Published By Parables, 2018.

5. Bruce, F.F. and Harrison, *R.K. Illustrated Dictionary of the Bible.* Nashville, Tennessee: Thomas Nelson Publishers, 1986.

6. Allen, Dr. Bruce and Van Vlymen, Michael. *Translation By Faith.* Spokane, WA: Still Waters International Ministries, 2015.

7. Selvaraj, Sadhu Sundar. *The Maharishi of Mt. Kailash.*Chennai: Jesus Ministries, 2011.

8. Rountree, Anna. *The Heavens Opened.* Lake Mary, Florida: Creation House Publishing, 1999.

9. Selvaraj, Sadhu Sundar. *Last days Seven Horns Anointing*. Singapore: Jesus Ministries Pte Ltd, 2016

10. Baxter, Mary.*A Divine Revelation of Angels*. New Kensington, PA.: Whitaker House, 2003

11. Capps, Charles, and Capps, Annette. *Angels Knowing Their Purpose Releasing Their Power*. Tulsa Oklahoma: Harrison House, 1984.

Dawn of A New *E. R. A.*

Dr. Etienne M. Graves Jr.

CPSIA information can be obtained
at www.ICGtesting.com
Printed in the USA
BVHW040951260221
601177BV00010B/1060

9 781951 497019